radar

free
running

Paul Mason
and Sarah Eason

First published in 2011 by Wayland

Wayland
Hachette Children's Books
338 Euston Road
London NW1 3BH

Wayland Australia
Level 17/207 Kent Street
Sydney NSW 2000

Concept by Joyce Bentley

Commissioned by Debbie Foy and Rasha Elsaeed

Produced for Wayland by Calcium
Designer: Paul Myerscough
Editor: Sarah Eason

Photographer: Adam Lawrence

British Library Cataloguing in Publication Data

Mason, Paul, 1967–
   Free running.
   1. Running—Juvenile literature.
   2. Street life—Juvenile literature.
   I. Title II. Eason, Sarah.
   796.4'25-dc22

ISBN: 978 0 7502 6458 7

Printed in China

Wayland is a division of Hachette Children's Books, an Hachette UK company.

www.hachette.co.uk

Acknowledgements: Jon Bolton 3b, 30; Eleazar Castillo 6; Flickr: Geishaboy500 2–3, 12–13, 18t, 29tl, 29tr, Beth Jusino 23c, Eneas de Troya 23t; Shirley Foster 14–15; Parkour Alliance cover, 2t, 2r, 10–11, 21, 23b, 25, 26–27, 28b; Patrick De Perio: 2b, 12, 13, 29b; Rex Features: Sony Pics/Everett 2c, 8; Shutterstock: Galina Barskaya 16, Sergey Goruppa 1, 17, Radin Myroslav 7, SVLuma 18b, Brooke Whatnall 4–5.

cover stories

the**people**

the**moves**

the**talk**

FREE RUNNING

Free running is a thrilling, high-energy urban activity. It combines incredible athletic skills with gymnastics – but it doesn't take place on a running track or in a gym. Free runners run just about everywhere in cities or towns, from streets and parks to shopping centres and car parks. And they don't just run – they clear any obstacles they meet along the way with impressive leaps, vaults and somersaults.

NO ORDINARY RUNNERS

Many people run for exercise or enjoyment. They run along a street, a running track or in a park. Free runners run for exercise and fun, but they also perform amazing stunts as they run. Free running stunts are carried out as much for their wow-factor as for their purpose, which is to overcome an object. Most ordinary runners would not vault across a park bench because they saw an opportunity to try out an impressive move – a free runner would.

THE FREE RUNNING WAY

Free running is about moving through a space with complete ease. It is about moving your way, as you choose, with absolute freedom. That is why it is called free running.

What do you need to free run?

- Physical fitness
- Calm, focused mind
- Determination
- Nerves of steel
- Loose, comfortable clothes and a pair of trainers!

THE FREE RUNNING STORY

In the 1980s, in a Paris suburb called Lisses, a group of teenagers met. They began running together around the town – but this was no ordinary running. They thundered over roofs, leapt cat-like across gaps, vaulted over benches and somersaulted off walls. It was the start of a new way of running – and the start of something big...

David Belle's visionary style of running was the inspiration for parkour.

WHO WERE THE RUNNERS?

The runners were all young Frenchmen and included David Belle and Sébastien Foucan. They called themselves the Yamakasi, an African word meaning 'strong body, strong spirit, strong person'. They named their form of running parkour, which is French for 'the art of movement'.

THE BRILLIANT BELLE

David Belle was a brilliant gymnast and runner. His father, Raymond, had trained David as a child to run quickly and efficiently – taking on obstacles as challenges that could be overcome with impressive gymnastic moves. It was David's way of running, this new physical philosophy, that became parkour.

In the beginning...

The idea behind running in a free and superbly athletic way first came from a Frenchman named Georges Hébert. In the early twentieth century, he taught a type of running and jumping over objects without fear to soldiers in the French army. It was this method of physical training that inspired Raymond Belle, and in turn David Belle.

FREE RUNNING STARTS

The Yamakasi eventually broke up. Members of the group, including David and Sébastien, carried on practising parkour. Sébastien began to introduce more and more stunts to his runs. These stunts weren't all about efficiency, but were used to make a beautiful movement or just for fun.

FREE RUNNING GETS ITS NAME

In 2003 Sébastien starred in a film documentary called *Jump London*, in which he and a small group of fellow runners ran across historic London buildings. It was then that Sébastien's form of parkour was given a name – free running.

SÉBASTIEN FOUCAN

THE FIRST FREE RUNNER

THE STATS

Name: Sébastien Foucan
Born: 24 May 1974
Place of birth: Paris, France
Personal life: Married with one daughter
Job: Free runner and actor

EARLY DAYS

Like all children, the young Sébastien Foucan loved running, jumping and climbing. As he grew older, Sébastien's runs became more challenging and his jumps bigger and more breathtaking. When he was 15 years old, Sébastien's life changed forever when he met David Belle through a group of mutual friends. The group shared a love of a new form of running they called parkour. They became the Yamakasi.

One of the many amazing free running stunts Sébastien performed in *Casino Royale.*

WORD SPREADS

In 2001 Sébastien starred with the Yamakasi in their own parkour film called *Yamâkasi – Les samouraïs des temps modernes*, meaning 'samurai of the modern age'. The film made Sébastien and other members of the Yamakasi famous across France. Sébastien hit the big screen again in 2003, when he starred in the sensational *Jump London* film. The incredible footage turned Sébastien into an overnight sensation in the UK.

ON TOUR WITH MADONNA

In 2005, Madonna invited Sébastien to perform in the music video for her single *Jump*. Impressed with Sébastien's free running style, Madonna then asked him to star on stage with her as a dancer and free runner during her *Confessions* tour in 2006.

THE BOND VILLAIN

It was in 2006 that free running really captured the public's imagination when Sébastien appeared in the Bond film *Casino Royale*. He starred as the 'baddie' character Mollaka, and performed a jaw-dropping free running chase scene to open the film. Film crowds gasped in amazement as they watched Sébastien free run – most people had never seen anything like it. The film made Sébastien a superstar and introduced the world to free running…

Type 'Sébastien Foucan Casino Royale' into www.youtube.com to watch his amazing chase scene!

Career highlights

2007 helped to develop the world's first free running shoe with sportswear manufacturer K-Swiss

2008 starred in the trailer for the action adventure video game *Mirror's Edge*

2009 starred in the action film *The Tournament*. Foucan featured as the character Anton Bogart, a French free running master

DOWNWARD RAIL PRECISION

Downward rail precision is a challenging move used by free runners to jump from a high point onto a narrow object, such as a railing. This move is for experienced free runners only!

1

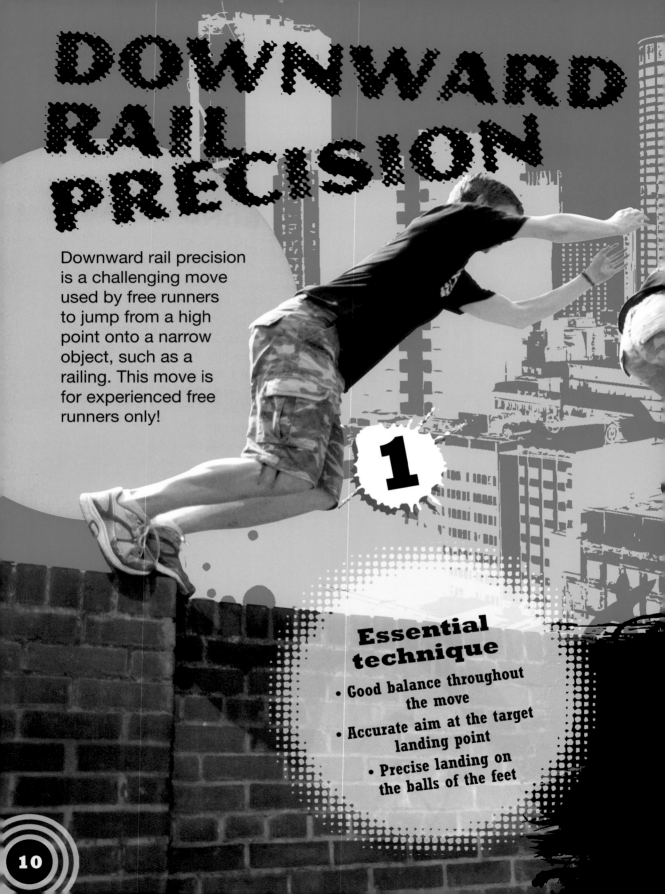

Essential technique

- Good balance throughout the move
- Accurate aim at the target landing point
- Precise landing on the balls of the feet

HOW IT'S DONE

1. The runner jumps as high as possible, extending the arms forward.
2. The runner's legs are tucked up and under the body to gain maximum height. At the highest point of the jump, the runner stretches the legs towards the landing point.
3. On landing, the runner places the feet on the rail. The legs are bent to take the impact of the jump. Superb balancing skills are required by the runner to hold a firm position on the rail before leaping off.

WHY DO IT?

By landing on a midway surface such as a railing, runners break the jump from a high point to the ground. Free runners can also use the move to spring off the midway surface onto another object.

IS FREE RUNNING OK?

Many people believe that free running is an amazing form of exercise, a philosophy and way of life. They say:

FOR

1. Free running is cheap! The only equipment needed is a pair of running shoes.
2. Free runners can run anywhere – parks, playgrounds and city streets are free running gyms.
3. People can run to work, school or college. That makes it a cheap and eco-friendly form of transport.
4. Free running is a whole body workout and a great way to stay fit.
5. Young free runners can hang out together while doing something healthy.
6. The exercise helps people to think positively and 'connect' with their surroundings.
7. There are no rules. Free running philosophy encourages people to find their own running style.

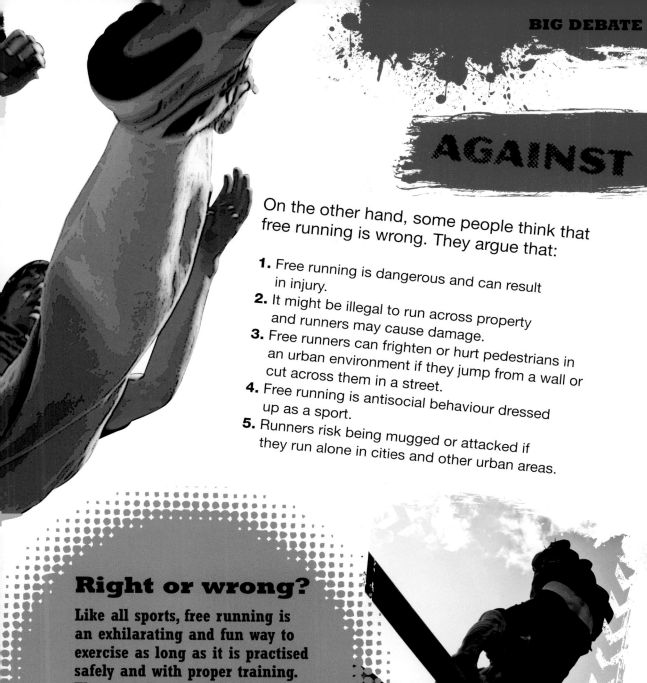

AGAINST

On the other hand, some people think that free running is wrong. They argue that:

1. Free running is dangerous and can result in injury.
2. It might be illegal to run across property and runners may cause damage.
3. Free runners can frighten or hurt pedestrians in an urban environment if they jump from a wall or cut across them in a street.
4. Free running is antisocial behaviour dressed up as a sport.
5. Runners risk being mugged or attacked if they run alone in cities and other urban areas.

Right or wrong?

Like all sports, free running is an exhilarating and fun way to exercise as long as it is practised safely and with proper training. The sport is best learned under the supervision of a free running instructor or group. There are also many public places such as parks where people can run without damaging property.

WILL FOSTER

THE STATS

Name: Will Foster
Born: 22 February 1996
Place of birth: UK
Nationality: British
Job: Schoolboy, free runner and child actor

STARTING OUT

Will's free running career started when a teacher showed his class a free running DVD instead of teaching them maths! The DVD starred the awesome free runner Sébastien Foucan. Will was amazed by Sébastien's stunts and wanted to try out free running. He began running shortly after watching the film – and caught the buzz. He was just 10 years old.

GLOSSARY

GLOSSARY

antisocial
a type of behaviour that upsets other people

documentary
a film recording that explains or examines a subject

evolution
a way of adapting or changing over time in order to survive

formidable
something or someone who inspires great respect

illegal
something that is against the law

impact
the force with which something hits or is hit

mutual
shared

philosophy
way of thinking

revolutionary
someone who radically changes something

rotation
to roll or spin in a complete circle

rush
a thrill or 'buzz'

samurai
an ancient Japanese warrior

vert
curved wall in a skatepark that bikers and skateboarders use to perform stunts

17

TO DO:
- move like an animal...
- be fluid like water...
- find your own balance...

THE URBAN PLAYGROUND

In cities across the world an army of athletes are taking to the streets. They swarm over monuments and pound along pavements. Who are these urban revolutionaries? They are free runners.

EVERYONE'S TALKING ABOUT IT

Since the 1990s, free running has grown in popularity to become one of the most talked about of all urban activities. It has taken its place alongside other hip and cutting-edge city sports such as skateboarding and BMX riding – in fact, head to any skatepark these days and you are as likely to see a free runner tricking on a vert as you are to see a skater or biker trying out a stunt. So, what is it about this thrill-seeking urban sport that makes it so popular?

EVOLUTION OR REVOLUTION?

Sébastien Foucan, one of the world's leading free runners, describes free running as an 'evolution' in which runners find their own way as they run. Could it be this freedom of movement, this lack of rules, that appeals to runners? Perhaps free running offers people a way to shake off the stress of their everyday lives. After all, to a free runner a city's boundaries and walls are a playground where they can swing, jump and vault. It is a world away from the 9-to-5 of office life.

A WAY OUT

Free runners push themselves constantly, refusing to accept that an object is too high or too far away to jump. Is it this ability to overcome enormous physical challenges, that makes free runners feel alive and not just a cog in a machine? Free running is more than just a way of running, it is a way of busting through the stress of modern life to feel free and alive again. It is the ultimate urban great escape.

Is free running the answer to the stress of modern life and city living?

URBAN RUNNER

LUKMAN HUSSIN'S STORY

When I was a kid, I was always running, jumping and climbing things, like most children. As I got older, I grew out of it and got into other things – until I went to a party that changed my life forever.

I met a free runner there who was completely into his running, really addicted. I could see the buzz he got from free running and it made me want to try it out myself. A couple of days later, we went for my first free running session. We only tried basic moves – but the free running bug hit me straight away. I was hooked!

Next I started training a lot and running with a free running group. As I trained more, I got faster and stronger, and my technique got better and better. I knew I could do more, so I started to try out new and harder tricks and ran in more challenging places. I kept pushing myself harder – to the limits. My body ached from all the training and I badly strained my muscles on one session. I was much more careful about taking risks after that.

Since I started free running I've put on free running demonstrations for charities and I've shown off my acrobatic skills in a stage play called *The Masked Man*. I've made my own free running short films and I've even starred in the circus tour, *No Fit State Circus*.

I'm really glad I went to that party and started free running – it's the best thing I've ever done..

– Lukman –

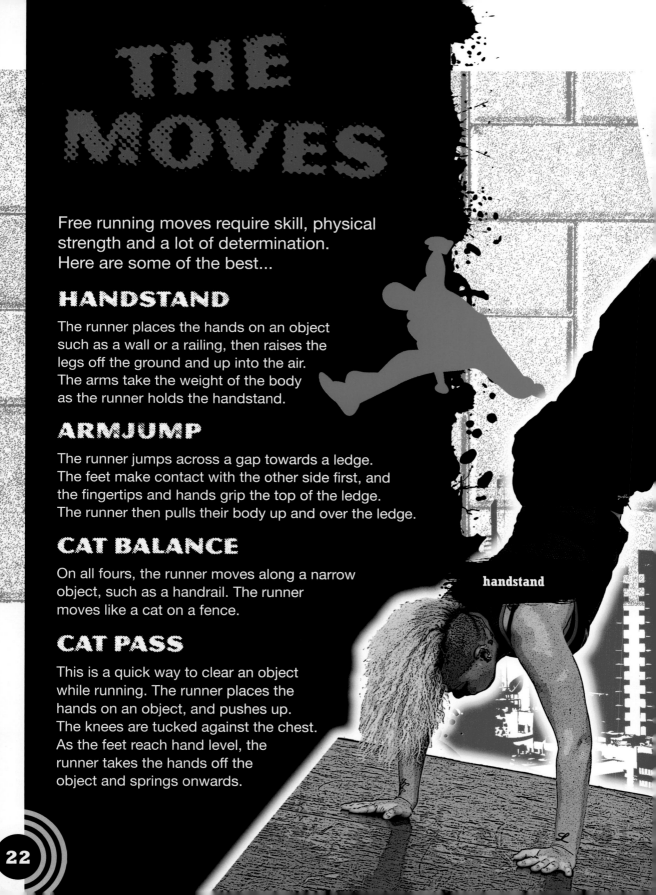

THE MOVES

Free running moves require skill, physical strength and a lot of determination. Here are some of the best...

HANDSTAND

The runner places the hands on an object such as a wall or a railing, then raises the legs off the ground and up into the air. The arms take the weight of the body as the runner holds the handstand.

ARMJUMP

The runner jumps across a gap towards a ledge. The feet make contact with the other side first, and the fingertips and hands grip the top of the ledge. The runner then pulls their body up and over the ledge.

CAT BALANCE

On all fours, the runner moves along a narrow object, such as a handrail. The runner moves like a cat on a fence.

CAT PASS

This is a quick way to clear an object while running. The runner places the hands on an object, and pushes up. The knees are tucked against the chest. As the feet reach hand level, the runner takes the hands off the object and springs onwards.

handstand

armjump

cat balance

cat pass

Type 'free running cat balance' into www.youtube.com to see footage of this amazing move!

23

MATTHEW DICKERSON

Matthew is a leading UK free runner, coach and all-round expert on free running. Radar asks him the questions you want to know!

When you free run, you compete against yourself alone – you don't worry about beating anyone else. You just challenge yourself. I love that side of it.

Do you need training to start free running?

If you want to start free running, it's best to find a coach. That way you'll learn how to run safely and a coach can also help you work on your own style.

Is it best to run alone or in a group?

Start off running as part of a group so you can ask other free runners for advice or help. You'll also make great friends. It's best to wait until you've been running for a while before going it alone.

Where are the best places to run?

Great running places have plenty of open space, but also fun obstacles such as park benches or walls. You can try out some great tricks on these. Stick to the low walls to start with!

Have you ever injured yourself or broken a bone while free running?

Not so far! I think if you are really careful and you perfect your technique you can run safely without hurting yourself.

What are your top five free running tips?

1. Keep yourself fit.
2. Practise, practise, practise!
3. Talk to other free runners for advice and inspiration.
4. Join a free running club.
5. Keep running and don't give up!

SIDE FLIP

The side flip is a breathtaking side somersault. This move is used to power over obstacles with traffic-stopping effect!

3

4

Essential technique

- Super-fast run into the move
- Tight posture held during rotation
- Accurate landing

HOW IT'S DONE

1. The runner runs hard and fast to the take-off point to avoid any hesitant steps known as 'stutter steps'.

2. The runner jumps into the air from the take-off point. The arms are stretched forward.

3. The legs are pulled up and knees tucked into the chest. The body rotates sideways through the air.

4. The runner's legs extend towards the landing point. The arms are outstretched to help maintain balance.

WHY DO IT?

The side flip is an impressively acrobatic move used to clear low objects such as steps, small walls and fences. The move allows runners to travel swiftly over obstacles without touching the ground and so avoid losing speed.

MORE MOVES

The most exhilarating free running stunts involve spins, vaults, backflips and somersaults.

PRECISION

A precision move is used to jump from one object to another, landing on the balls of the feet. For landing, the arms and legs come forwards.

precision

SPEED VAULT

This move is used to jump over a low wall. The free runner runs towards the wall, leans forward and places one hand on the wall. The runner then lifts the body to vault sideways over the wall.

REVERSE PALM SPIN

In this move, the free runner jumps upwards towards a wall. They place one hand on the wall, then flip over the hand to land on the ground.

TACK BACK

The runner jumps towards a wall, then uses the hands and feet to push back off the wall and land elsewhere.

speed vault

LAYOUT BACK TUCK

The free runner throws themselves backwards off an object such as a roof or wall. As they travel through the air, they flip themselves upright and land on the feet.

reverse palm spin

tack back

Type 'free running palm spin' into www.youtube.com to see footage of this amazing move!

layout back tuck

THE JAM

All eyes are on you. Your hands are grazed raw, your feet are blistered, you drip with sweat and your muscles shake with the strain of running, pulling, leaping and vaulting. You've already tested your body to its limits, but now it's your turn to perform yet another spectacular move in front of a crowd of incredible free runners. And you just can't wait! Welcome to a free running jam…

ADRENALIN JUNKIES

All around you see free runners tricking – side flipping over walls, vaulting through the air and performing incredible, arm-quivering handstands on super-high walls and railings. You hear the cheers from the crowd every time a runner takes their turn to trick, and the whoops of approval when they showcase their stunt.

NO LIMITS

You can feel the wall beneath your feet, your muscles are tense and taut and your mouth is dry. It's time. You bend your legs and push up into the air, twisting and turning. Faces are blurred, you see the bricks of the wall spin past, then the sand coming up to meet you. Your feet plunge into the ground and you bend over into a roll. Your body buzzes with a feeling like no other – it's the free running rush.

What's the buzz?

When a free runner performs a trick a hormone called adrenalin rushes through their body. Known as a 'rush', this hormone surge fills the runner with energy.

START RUNNING

People to talk to

Want to start free running? Then get your trainers on and start talking to the people who can help. There are lots of organisations that can get you off the sofa and into free running!

Parkour Alliance

Matthew Dickerson is the founder of Parkour Alliance. Check out the Alliance's courses and running group: **www.norwich-parkour.co.uk**

Parkour Generations

Find courses and jam sessions at: **www.parkourgenerations.com**

American Parkour

Start free running in the US with this leading parkour group. Their website is packed with information and ideas: **www.americanparkour.com**

Urban Freeflow

Meet other free runners on facebook at: **www.facebook. com/urbanfreeflow**

APPs & DVDs

Check out the apps *iTraceur* and *Let's Parkour Pro* at: **www.itunes.com**

Put on the *Jump London* DVD – the ultimate free running film.

INDEX